CW00506406

INTERMITTENT FASTING COOKBOOK

Discover Mouth-Watering, Simple and Fast Recipes tailored for the IF Diet

|Lose Weight, Stay Healthy and Live Longer |

TERESA MOORE

Copyright © 2020 Teresa Moore

All rights reserved.

"THE STARTING POINT OF ALL ACHIEVEMENTS IS DESIRE"
NAPOLEON HILL

CONTENTS

FOODS TO EAT | FOODS TO AVOID WHEN FOLLOWING AN INTERMITTENT FASTING REGIME

Health is wealth. It is portrayed as the ideal prosperity of an individual whether it is physical or mental in nature. Remaining fit and sound advances an uplifting viewpoint and keeps up an energetic and dynamic manner. In addition to the fact that it preserves youth, it additionally extends our life. Presently, one of the most creative approaches to keep oneself sound and fit is through intermittent fasting. On the off chance you need to protect your health, youth and the essentialness of your being; at that point, intermittent fasting ought to be checked out.

Intermittent fasting, as portrayed today, is one of the least expensive fasting diets to shed pounds. It doesn't require some other instruments, for example, pills or meds, nor does it involve any costly exercise center hardware. All it essentially asks is severe and harsh control to fasting. Intermittent fasting, by definition, implies the guideline of food consumption by not ingesting anything between major meals. Additionally, by the word intermittent, it follows that a successive request for an eating plan must be found.

There's an assumption among specialists that the premise on how intermittent fasting actually functions can be clarified by reason of life structures and physiology; or the investigation of the organ and organ frameworks in connection to their capacities inside our bodies. As clarified by experts, for example, doctors, inside our brain stem lies the seat of satiety, appetite, and thirst called the nerve center. The nerve center is an unpredictable, diverse organ that actually tells our body when to want to eat.

Henceforth, if there be any craving to drink or eat; the nerve center is the one liable for such activity. In this way, whenever left undeveloped and left to do alone, satiety and appetite will increase to colossal extents.

When this occurs, the desire to drink or eat will likewise be amplified. Obviously, there is no threat or hazard to eating. There is literally nothing amiss with that; be that as it may, the nature of the food admission we eat likewise decides the condition of health among people. Moreover, if an individual constantly ingests foods that are not nutritious, say the ones we find in fast food sources or cafeterias; and it's done in enormous sums, health is influenced. Uncontrolled eating can prompt a large group of ailments, for example, diabetes, hypertension, cardiovascular or heart issues and obesity.

The most ideal approach to begin your fasting is to deliberately design your meals. Intermittent fasting works best if it is done routinely and constantly. This type of fasting diet to get more fit must be done as per the eagerness of the member; and must be taught so as to accomplish the ideal impacts. Besides fasting, if you intend to get thinner, the amount of caloric admission should likewise be considered. Thus, besides cautiously arranging the intermittent meals, the amount of calories should likewise be thought about.

Joining the two methodologies won't simply make you thin; it will assist you with getting to the weight you've constantly needed. In addition, preparing your nerve center to eat intermittently will hugely affect your inclination to eat or drink, which would prompt limiting your undesirable dietary habits.

Foods to eat

There are no good and bad foods fundamentally, however, on the other hand, eating only lousy food won't be beneficial for you. You should attempt to keep the food in your eating regimen sensible and adjusted with the goal that you don't fix all your hard work fasting.

A method for doing this is to think about the kinds of foods you ought to maintain a strategic distance from.

You may be lured to go for sugary foods or refined carbs to give you momentary delight. Be that as it may, these processed bad foods are empty fuel that won't furnish your fasting body with the supplements it needs and will probably leave you feeling eager and touchy.

So, when you are moving toward an intermittent fast, what are the best foods to have in your refrigerator and pantries?

1. Whole grains

Whole grains are brimming with significant fiber and protein and go far to support your digestion. They are a perfect substitution for refined carbs and help towards a solid stomach related framework as well.

2. Fish

Fish is rich in sound fats and protein which are basic to building and restoring your body during intermittent fasting. It additionally contains vitamin D which assists with combatting any decrease in the mental capacity that is a significant regular symptom of an intermittent fasting diet, henceforth why fish is normally alluded to as 'mind food'.

3. Probiotics

Fasting can agitate the sensitive equalization of microscopic organisms in your gut, and this can bring about reactions like constipation. Probiotic foods like yogurt, kefir, and kraut can enable your gut to keep up its equalization when fasting.

4. Eggs

We as a whole realize eggs are stuffed with protein, yet one of the genuine points of interest of eggs in your intermittent fasting diet is that eggs are extremely adaptable. You aren't restricted to hard-boiled eggs; however, they make a helpful tidbit that is prepared in minutes when you need it. They can be mixed and made in an entire assortment of ways with the goal that you're not eating a similar meal twice.

5. Nuts

Nuts do have a higher carbohydrate level; however, they are brimming with the great sorts of fat you need just like protein. They function admirably as a filling snack in modest quantities, and can likewise be added to other beautiful plates, for example, servings of mixed greens and yogurts when you want to mix things up.

6. Berries

Vitamin C is basic for your insusceptible framework, and organic products, for example, strawberries or blueberries can give all of what your everyday prerequisite demands, alongside flavonoids. What's more, we should not overlook your sweet tooth, which will shout to you when you bring down your calorie intake. Berries are a great way to address the sugar cravings without giving up your eating routine.

7. Beans and vegetables

When you are intermittently fasting, you should be eating foods that give you the energy to get past the fasting timeframes. An extraordinary option in contrast to refined carbs are beans, vegetables, peas, lentils, and chickpeas that have been demonstrated to help reduce your body weight without pushing your calorie limit. Marvelous!

8. Green leafy vegetables

These veggies are a great way to get your body the sustenance it needs sensibly. What's more, more than anything, vegetables are a wonderful source of fiber that will leave you feeling full for longer just as keeping your insides and digestion working.

Intermittent fasting is tied in with restricting when you eat more than it is about what you eat. Yet, whenever the fateful opening strikes it's shrewd to fuel up on the things your body needs rather than sugary cravings. It's not about pain or starvation, and with our rundown of best foods, you can mix and match and keep those intermittent meals fascinating.

Foods to avoid

1. Sugar

When individuals catch wind of drinking herbal tea, they right away consider sugars. Shouldn't something be said about tea with honey? Tea with sugar? What about Arnold Palmer?

However, in light of the fact that tea with honey looks the same doesn't mean it's equal to plain herbal tea once it's in your body. Sweetened tea is simply unadulterated basic sugars, with no fiber or fat to hinder its retention. The outcome is equivalent to if you were to eat a bunch of M&Ms: a brisk spike in glucose, a relating arrival of insulin, and a conclusion to the adequacy of your fasting period. Honey has some supportive properties, yet not while fasting.

Curiously enough, late studies have indicated that zero-calorie sugars can likewise trigger the arrival of insulin. This implies it's likewise imperative to avoid sucralose, stevia, and fake sugars while fasting. In case you're truly attached to your sweetened beverages, drink them during meals, not during your fasting period.

2. Caffeine

Caffeine, found in espresso, dark tea, and green tea, can likewise be hazardous while fasting. This comes as amazement to numerous individuals. All things considered, in case you're maintaining a strategic distance from food and sugar, why not get a synthetic lift to assist you with livening up?

Caffeine will liven you up, yet the impact is temporary. Caffeine obstructs the receptors for adenosine, the substance in your body that causes you to feel drowsy. Be that as it may, the synthetic substances don't leave since caffeine is making your body overlook them. This implies when the caffeine has worn off, you regularly crash, and hard. Individuals with a caffeine addiction understand this tendency well. Join that with a fast, and the subsequent descend can leave you incapable of working.

Indeed, even people who commonly drink espresso with their morning meal can encounter symptoms from drinking it on an empty stomach, including physical butterflies, mood swings, acid reflux, and indigestion. (Sad to report, decaf espresso isn't useful for your stomach either.) Add to that the way that numerous individuals see espresso and stimulated tea as unpleasant and unpalatable without cream, sugar, or another added substance. So, in case, you're asking yourself, "how would I drink espresso while on a fast?" The basic answer is its best just to disregard it while fasting.

Calories

This ought to be truly self-evident, yet calories can be subtle. Packaged waters showcased towards competitors regularly contain calories, as do clear soups that numerous individuals consider to be water's nearby cousin. Chewing gum contains calories (truly, even the juice from chewing it, not including the gum itself), and packaged and bundled teas regularly do too.

Vitamins and other supplements commonly have a few calories as well; in case you're fasting, leave these off until your planned feast. Cough drops and other drugs likewise come with included calories. In case you're sick enough to need drugs, you should most likely postpone fasting until you have recouped.

This doesn't imply that medications and supplements have no spot in your life if you take an interest in intermittent fasting. It's ideal, however, if you can plan to take them with meals. Obviously, if your doctor has you on a severe timetable with your drug, follow your primary care physician's rules. Getting over a disease is a higher priority than any fasting daily exercise.

Intermittent fasting can be an awesome weight reduction device

With a little planning, arranging, and sound judgment, intermittent fasting can remove weight reduction from the field of "perhaps sometime in the not so distant future" and into the real world. For more data about intermittent fasting, grab a free copy of the Intermittent Fasting Cheat Sheet. Quit fighting with your body and start working with it to get more fit and turn into the strong individual you were constantly intended to be.

CHAPTER TWO

DELICIOUS AND HEALTHY RECIPES FOR INTERMITTENT FASTING

If you've as of late bounced onto the Intermittent fasting temporary fad, you should be pondering about the foods you can eat. In this subchapter, we'll disseminate a couple of basic Intermittent Fasting recipes you can evaluate whenever you cook. Likewise, we've included Intermittent Fasting veggie-lover plans for those of you who decide to abandon meat!

Intermittent fasting recipes

As it is ordinarily stated, breakfast is the most significant meal of the day. What's more, this is particularly so since it will be the meal you break your fast. Here are some nutritious Intermittent Fasting Breakfast, Lunch, Dinner, Dessert, and Snacks recipes you can evaluate whenever you're in the kitchen.

Breakfast

Chinese-Style Zucchini with Ginger

Nutritional Facts

Servings per container	10
Prep Total	10 min
Serving Size 2/3 cup (55g)	
Amount per serving	
Calories	20
	% Daily Value
Total Fat 8g	6%
Saturated Fat 1g	2%
Trans Fat 0g	-
Cholesterol	0%
Sodium 160mg	9%
Total Carbohydrate 37g	50%
Dietary Fiber 4g	2
Total Sugar 12g	-
Protein 3g	

Vitamin C 2mcg	1%
Calcium 260mg	8%
Iron 8mg	17%
Potassium 235mg	8%

Ingredients

- 1 teaspoon oil
- 1 lb. zucchini cut into 1/4 inch slices
- 1/2 cup vegetarian broth
- 2 teaspoons light soy sauce
- 1 teaspoon dry sherry
- 1 teaspoon roasted sesame oil

Instructions:

- Heat a large wok or heavy skillet over high heat until very hot then add the oil. When the oil is hot, add the zucchini and ginger.
- Stir-fry 1 minute.
- Add the broth, soy sauce, and sherry.
- Stir-fry over high heat until the broth cooks down a bit and the zucchini is crisp-tender.
- Remove from the heat, sprinkle with sesame oil and serve

Breakfast Super Antioxidant Berry Smoothie

Nutritional Facts

Servings per container	**5**
Prep Total	10 min
Serving Size 4 cup (20g)	
Amount per serving	
Calories	20
	% Daily Value
Total Fat 2g	5%
Saturated Fat 2g	4%
Trans Fat 7g	-
Cholesterol	2%
Sodium 7mg	9%
Total Carbohydrate 20g	20%
Dietary Fiber 4g	20%
Total Sugar 12g	-
Protein 3g	
Vitamin C 2mcg	15%
Calcium 260mg	7%
Iron 8mg	4%

Potassium 235mg	1%

Ingredients

- 1 cup of filtered water
- 1 whole orange, peeled, de-seeded & cut into chunks
- 2 cups frozen raspberries or blackberries
- 1 Tablespoon goji berries
- 1 1/2 Tablespoons hemp seeds or plant-based protein powder
- 2 cups leafy greens (parsley, spinach, or kale)

Instructions:

- Blend on high until smooth
- Serve and drink immediately

Cucumber Tomato Surprise

Nutritional Facts

Servings per container	5
Prep Total	10 min
Serving Size 2/3 cup (55g)	
Amount per serving	
Calories	2
	% Daily Value
Total Fat 20g	17%
Saturated Fat 2g	1%
Trans Fat 1.2g	-
Cholesterol	20%
Sodium 55mg	12%
Total Carbohydrate 14g	50%
Dietary Fiber 4g	8%
Total Sugar 2g	-
Protein 7g	
Vitamin C 2mcg	10%
Calcium 20mg	2%

Iron 1mg	5%
Potassium 210mg	7%

Ingredients

- Chopped 1 medium of tomato
- 1 small cucumber peeled in stripes and chopped
- 1 large avocado cut into cubes
- 1 half of a lemon or lime squeezed
- ½ tsp. Himalayan or Real salt
- 1 Teaspoon of original olive oil, MCT or coconut oil

Instructions:

- Mix everything together and enjoy
- This dish tastes even better after sitting for 40 – 60 minutes
- Blend into a soup if desired.

Avocado Nori Rolls

Nutritional Facts

Servings per container	10
Prep Total	10 min
Serving Size 2/3 cup (70g)	
Amount per serving	
Calories	15
	% Daily Value
Total Fat 2g	10%
Saturated Fat 1g	9%
Trans Fat 10g	-
Cholesterol	1%
Sodium 70mg	5%
Total Carbohydrate 22g	40%
Dietary Fiber 4g	2%
Total Sugar 12g	-
Protein 3g	
Vitamin C 2mcg	2%
Calcium 260mg	7%

Iron 8mg	2%
Potassium 235mg	4%

Ingredients

- 2 sheets of raw or toasted sushi nori
- 1 large Romaine leaf cut in half down the length of the spine
- 2 Teaspoons of spicy miso paste
- 1 avocado, peeled and sliced
- ½ red, yellow or orange bell pepper, julienned
- ½ cucumber, peeled, seeded and julienned
- ½ cup raw sauerkraut
- ½ carrot, beet or zucchini, shredded
- 1 cup alfalfa or favorite green sprouts
- 1 small bowl of water for sealing roll

Instructions:

- Place a sheet of nori on a sushi rolling mat or washcloth, lining it up at the end closest to you.
- Place the Romaine leaf on the edge of the nori with the spine closest to you.
- Spread Spicy Miso Paste on the Romaine
- Line the leaf with all ingredients in descending order, placing sprouts on last
- Roll the Nori sheet away from you tucking the ingredients in with your fingers and seal the roll with water or Spicy Miso Paste. Slice the roll into 6 or 8 rounds.

MAPLE GINGER PANCAKES

Nutritional Facts

Servings per container	4
Prep Total	10 min
Serving Size 2/3 cup (20g)	
Amount per serving	
Calories	20
	% Daily Value
Total Facts 10g	10%
Saturated Fat 0g	7%
Trans Fat 2g	-
Cholesterol	3%
Sodium 10mg	2%
Total Carbohydrate 7g	3%
Dietary Fiber 2g	4%
Total Sugar 1g	-
Protein 3g	
Vitamin C 2mcg	10%
Calcium 260mg	20%

Iron 8mg	30%
Potassium 235mg	6%

Ingredients

- 1 or 2 cups flour
- 1 tablespoonful baking powder
- 1/2 tablespoonful kosher salt
- 1/4 tablespoonful ground ginger
- 1/4 tablespoonful pumpkin pie spice
- 1/3 cup maple syrup
- 2/4 cup water
- Mix 1/4 cup + 1 tablespoonful crystallized ginger slices together

Instructions:

- In a neat bowl mix together the first five recipes
- Add flour with syrup with water and stir together, after that add in the chopped ginger & stir until-just-combined.
- Heat your frying pan and coat with a non-stick cooking spray
- Pour in 1/4 cup of the batter and allow it to heat until it forms bubbles. Allow to cook until browned
- Serve warm & topped with a slathering of vegan butter, a splash of maple syrup and garnished with chopped candied ginger.

Chewy Chocolate Chip Cookies

Nutritional Facts

Servings per container	10
Prep Total	10 min
Serving Size 2/3 cup (40g)	
Amount per serving	
Calories	10
	% Daily Value
Total Fat 10g	2%
Saturated Fat 1g	5%
Trans Fat 0g	-
Cholesterol	15%
Sodium 120mg	8%
Total Carbohydrate 21g	10%
Dietary Fiber 4g	1%
Total Sugar 1g	0%
Protein 6g	
Vitamin C 2mcg	7%
Calcium 210mg	51%

Iron 8mg	1%
Potassium 235mg	10%

Ingredients

- 1 cup vegan butter, softened
- ½ cup white sugar
- ½ cup brown sugar
- ¼ cup dairy-free milk
- 1 teaspoon vanilla
- 2 ¼ cups flour
- ½ teaspoon salt
- 1 teaspoon baking soda
- 12 ounces dairy-free chocolate chips

Instructions:

- Preheat oven to 350°F.
- In a large bowl, mix the butter, white sugar, and brown sugar until light and fluffy. Slowly stir in the dairy-free milk and then add the vanilla to make a creamy mixture.
- In a separate bowl, combine the flour, salt, and baking soda.
- You need to add this dry mixture to the liquid mixture and stir it well. Fold in the chocolate chips.
- Drop a small spoonful of the batter onto non-stick cookie sheets and bake for 9 minutes.

Benedict Eggs

TIME: 20 MINUTES

Nutritional Facts

- Calories: 624
- Total fat: 53.9g
- Carbohydrates: 1.8g
- Net carbohydrates 1.8g
- Fiber: 0g
- Protein: 32.6g

Ingredients

FOR THE HOLLANDAISE SAUCE

- 2 eggs
- 1 1/2 teaspoons freshly squeezed lemon juice
- 1/4 cup butter, melted
- 1/4 teaspoon salt

FOR THE EGGS

- 4 slices of bacon
- 1 teaspoon of vinegar
- 4 eggs

Preparation

- Make the hollandaise sauce
- In a large bowl, beat two eggs and the lemon juice together vigorously until you get a solid whole and almost double in volume.
- Fill a large frying pan with 2.5 cm of water and heat until it simmers. Reduce the heat to medium.
- Wear an oven glove and hold the bowl with the eggs above the water and make sure it does not touch the water. Beat the mixture for about 3 minutes and make sure you do not mix the eggs.
- Slowly add the butter to the egg mixture and keep beating until thick, about 2 minutes.
- Stir in the salt.
- Stir the sauce until it has cooled.
- Make the eggs
- Pour the water from the pan and place it over medium heat. Place the bacon in the pan. Bake for 3 minutes per side. Transfer the bacon onto paper towels.
- Add the vinegar and apply over low heat to a medium-sized pan, half-full of water.
- Carefully break the eggs in the water and be careful not to break the yolks. Turn the heat to low to medium low. Cook for 3 to 4 minutes.
- Remove the eggs. Drain them and set them aside.

To serve

- Break bacon in half. Place two halves on a plate and garnish with an egg. Repeat with 2 more halves and another egg.
- Cover with hollandaise sauce.
- Repeat with the remaining bacon and the eggs for the second portion.

Scottish Eggs

TIME: 45 MINUTES

Nutritional Facts

- Calories: 258
- Total fat: 20.5g
- Carbohydrates: 14.2g
- Net carbohydrates 1g
- Fiber: 0g
- Protein: 16.7g

Ingredients

- 1/2 cup breakfast sausage
- 1/2 teaspoon garlic powder
- 1/4 teaspoon salt
- 1/8 teaspoon freshly ground black pepper
- 2 hard-boiled eggs, peeled

Preparation

- Preheat the oven to 200 ° C.
- Mix the sausage, garlic powder, salt and pepper in a medium bowl. Shape the sausage into two balls.

- Flatten each ball on a piece of baking paper into a 0.8 cm thick pastry.
- Place a hard-boiled egg in the center of each pie and carefully shape the sausage around the egg.
- Place the sausage-covered eggs on a non-greased baking sheet and place it in the preheated oven.
- Bake for 25 minutes. Allow to cool for 5 minutes and serve.
- EXTRA: Breakfast sausage is a typical American type of pork sausage and you can use something like sausages

Biscuits in Sausage gravy

TIME: 50 MINUTES

Nutritional Facts

- Calories: 559
- Total fat: 48.5g
- Carbohydrates: 14.2g
- Net carbohydrates 8.2g
- Fiber: 6g
- Protein: 14.6g

Ingredients

FOR THE Biscuits

- 1⁄2 cup coconut flour
- 1⁄2 cup almond flour
- 2 teaspoons baking powder
- 1 teaspoon garlic powder
- 1⁄2 teaspoon onion powder
- 1⁄2 teaspoon salt
- 1⁄2 cup grated Cheddar cheese
- 1/4 cup butter, melted
- 4 eggs

- 3/4 cup sour cream

For SAUSAGE Gravy

- 450 grams ground breakfast sausage
- 1 teaspoon finely chopped garlic
- 1 tablespoon almond flour
- 1 1/2 cup unsweetened almond milk
- 1/2 cup heavy (whipped) cream
- 1 1/2 teaspoon freshly ground black pepper
- 1/2 teaspoon salt

Preparation

- Preheat the oven to 180 ° C
- Cover a baking sheet with baking paper.
- In a large bowl, mix coconut flour, almond flour, baking powder, garlic powder, onion powder, and salt. Slowly stir in the Cheddar cheese.
- Make a pit in the middle of the dry ingredients before adding the wet ingredients.
- Add the melted butter, eggs and sour cream in this pit. Fold together until dough is formed.
- Use a spoon to drop biscuits onto the prepared baking sheet, place them 2.5 cm apart.
- Bake the cookies for 20 minutes or until they are firm and light brown.

Preparation of the sausage gravy

- Heat a large pan over medium heat. Add the ground sausage, open it with a spoon and bake it brown on all sides.
- Add the chopped garlic when the sausage is brown. Cook for 1 minute.

- If the garlic is fragrant, sprinkle the almond flour over it. Turn the heat low to medium low. Allow the almond flour to blend into the fat to develop a light roux, stirring constantly, for about 5 minutes.
- Slowly add the almond milk to the roux, stirring constantly.
- Add the whipped cream. Increase the temperature to medium - high, stir and reduce the mixture for 3 minutes.
- Turn the heat to low to medium low. Add the pepper and salt. Stir for 1 minute.
- Check the biscuits and remove the baking sheet from the oven when you're done. Let the biscuits cool for 5 minutes.
- Reduce the heat again under the sausage gravy to low. Simmer while the biscuits cool.
- Once the biscuits cool, serve 1 per person and garnish with a ⅓ cup of gravy.

Portobello, Sausage and Cheese "Breakfast Burger"

TIME: 25 MINUTES

Nutritional Facts

- Calories: 504
- Total fat: 41.1g
- Carbohydrates: 10.1g
- Net carbohydrates 7g
- Fiber: 3.1g
- Protein: 23.8g

Ingredients

- 1 tablespoon olive oil
- 2 Portobello mushrooms, stalk removed
- 1/4 cup breakfast sausage
- 2 (50 grams) slices of Cheddar cheese

Preparation

- Heat the olive oil for 1 minute in a medium-sized non-stick frying pan over medium heat.
- Place the mushrooms in the hot oil, with the convex side up. Bake for about 5 minutes per side, or until browned.

- Heat another medium-sized frying pan over medium heat.

- Form the breakfast sausage into a 1 cm thick pastry. Place it in the center of the heated pan. Bake for 4 to 5 minutes. Turn and bake for another 2 to 3 minutes.

- When the sausage is almost ready, turn down the heat. Garnish the burger with the Cheddar cheese. Cook until the cheese melts.

- Transfer the mushrooms from the skillet to a plate.

- Place the cheese-covered pie on one mushroom. Cover with the remaining mushroom cap and serve.

Cinnamon Muffins with Butter Frosting

TIME: 50 MINUTES

Nutritional Facts

- Calories: 225
- Total fat: 18.5g
- Carbohydrates: 6.2g
- Net carbohydrates 3.1g
- Fiber: 3.1g
- Protein: 5.3g

Ingredients

FOR CINNAMON MUFFINS

- 1 cup almond flour
- 1/2 cup coconut flour
- 2 teaspoons baking powder
- 1/4 cup erythritol or another sugar substitute, such as stevia
- 6 eggs
- 1/2 cup butter, melted
- 1/2 cup sparkling water
- 1 teaspoon pure vanilla extract
- 1 1/2 tablespoons cinnamon

FOR ICE CREAM Glaze

- 1 pack of cream cheese, at room temperature
- 1 tablespoon of sour cream
- 1/2 teaspoon of pure vanilla extract

Preparation of muffins

- Preheat the oven to 180 ° C.
- In a medium bowl, beat together the almond flour, coconut flour, baking powder and erythritol.
- Beat the eggs in a large bowl. Add the melted butter, sparkling water and vanilla. Beat to combine.
- Add the dry ingredients to the wet ingredients. Mix well.
- Put the batter evenly in a frying pan. Garnish each muffin with an equal amount of cinnamon.
- Stir the cinnamon through the batter with a toothpick.
- Place the cup form in the preheated oven. Bake for 20 to 25 minutes or until golden brown.
- Remove the pan from the oven and cool the muffins in the pan for 5 to 10 minutes.

- **Preparation of the Cream Cheese Glaze**
- In a medium bowl, mix cream cheese, sour cream and vanilla. Cool until needed. Spread evenly over the muffins before serving.

Almond flour Pancakes

TIME: 35 MINUTES

Nutritional Facts

- Calories: 383
- Total fat: 34g
- Carbohydrates: 7.9g
- Net carbohydrates 3.9g
- Fiber: 4g
- Protein: 3.8g

Ingredients

- 1 cup almond flour
- 1 tablespoon stevia or another sugar substitute
- 1/4 teaspoon salt
- 1 teaspoon baking powder
- 2 eggs
- 1⁄8 cup heavy (whipped) cream
- 1⁄8 cup sparkling water
- 1⁄2 teaspoon pure vanilla extract
- 2 tablespoons coconut oil, melted
- Baking spray for grill plate (plancha)

Preparation

- Heat a grill plate over medium heat.

- In a large bowl, mix almond flour, stevia, salt and baking powder.

- Make a small hole in the middle of the dry ingredients. Add the eggs, heavy cream, sparkling water, vanilla and coconut oil. Mix everything well.

- Spray the grill plate with baking spray. Pour the batter into the desired quantities on the grill plate. Bake the pancakes for 2 to 3 minutes, until you see small bubbles and then turn over. Bake for 1 to 2 minutes.

- Remove the pancakes from the baking sheet when they are ready. Repeat with the remaining batter.

Raspberry Scones

TIME: 35 MINUTES

Nutritional Facts

- Calories: 133
- Total fat: 8.6g
- Carbohydrates: 4g
- Net carbohydrates 2g
- Fiber: 2g
- Protein: 1.5g

Ingredients

- 1 cup almond flour
- 2 eggs, beaten
- 1/3 cup Splenda, stevia, or another sugar substitute
- 1 1/2 teaspoon pure vanilla extract
- 1 1/2 teaspoon baking powder
- 1/2 cup raspberries

Preparation

- Preheat the oven to 180 ° C.
- Cover a baking sheet with baking paper.

- In a large bowl, mix almond flour, eggs, Splenda, vanilla and baking powder. Mix well.

- Add the raspberries to the bowl and fold them in carefully.

- After the raspberries have been processed, scoop 2 to 3 tablespoons of batter, per scone, onto the baking tray lined with baking paper.

- Place the baking tray in the preheated oven. Bake for 15 minutes or until light brown.

- Remove the baking sheet from the oven. Place the scones on a rack to cool for 10 minutes.

INGREDIENT TIP: Depending on the size of the raspberries, you can cut the raspberries into two halves before adding them to the batter. By doing this the raspberry flavor is spread over the entire scone.

Waffles with whipped cream

TIME: 15 MINUTES

Nutritional Facts

- Calories: 420
- Total fat: 27.1g
- Carbohydrates: 15.7g
- Net carbohydrates: 6.5g
- Fiber: 9.2g
- Protein: 27g

Ingredients

FOR THE WAFFLES

- Baking spray for waffle iron
- 1/4 cup coconut flour 1/4 cup almond flour
- 1/4 cup flax flour
- 1 teaspoon baking powder
- 1 teaspoon stevia or another sugar substitute
- 1/4 teaspoon cinnamon
- 3/4 cup protein (about 3 proteins)
- 4 eggs
- 1 teaspoon pure vanilla extract

FOR THE WHIP CREAM

- 1/2 cup of heavy (whipped) cream
- 1 teaspoon of stevia or another sugar substitute

Preparation

- Prepare the waffles
- Heat the waffle maker to medium height.
- Cover with baking spray.
- In a large bowl, beat together the coconut flour, almond flour, flax flour, baking powder, stevia and cinnamon.
- Beat the egg whites in another medium-sized bowl until stiff peaks occur.
- Add the whole eggs and vanilla to the dry ingredients. Mix well.
- Carefully fold the whipped egg whites through the dry ingredients until completely absorbed.
- Pour the batter onto the preheated waffle maker. Bake according to the instructions of the waffle maker.

Prepare the whipped cream

- Beat the heavy cream in a medium bowl for 3 to 4 minutes, until thick.
- Add the stevia. Continue to beat until stiff peaks form, about 1 minute.
- Garnish the waffles with equal amounts of whipped cream and serve.

Cream cheese pancakes

TIME: 15 MINUTES

Nutritional Facts

- Calories: 327
- Total fat: 28.7g
- Carbohydrates: 2.5g
- Net carbohydrates: 2.5g
- Fiber: 0g
- Protein: 15.4g

Ingredients

- 1/4 cup cream cheese, at room temperature
- 2 eggs
- 1/2 teaspoon of stevia
- 1/4 teaspoon of nutmeg

Preparation

- Heat a grill plate (plancha) over medium heat.
- Place the cream cheese in a blender. Add the eggs, stevia and nutmeg. Mix until the batter is smooth.
- Slowly pour a small amount of batter onto the grill plate, about one-eighth cup per

pancake. The batter will be very thin and easy to spread.

- Bake the pancake a little longer than a minute before turning it over gently. Let it bake for another minute before you take it out of the pan.
- Repeat with the remaining batter.

Denver Omelet

TIME: 15 MINUTES

Nutritional Facts

- Calories: 429
- Total fat: 32.7g
- Carbohydrates: 9.1g
- Net carbohydrates: 6.9g
- Fiber: 2.2g
- Protein: 24.7g

Ingredients

- 1 tablespoon butter
- 1/4 cup chopped onion
- 1/4 cup chopped red pepper
- 1/4 cup chopped green pepper
- 1/2 teaspoon chopped garlic
- 1/4 cup cooked ham, cubed
- 2 eggs, beaten
- 1/4 teaspoon salt
- 1/8 teaspoon freshly ground black pepper
- 1/4 cup grated Cheddar cheese

Preparation

- Melt the butter in a medium-sized non-stick skillet over medium heat.
- Add the onion, red pepper, green pepper, garlic and ham. Cook until the ham is crispy, about 2 minutes.
- In a small bowl, beat the eggs with the salt and pepper. Pour the eggs into the pan with the vegetables and the ham. Reduce the heat to medium.
- Cook the eggs for 3 to 4 minutes. Turn the omelet. After turning around, sprinkle the upper half of the omelet with the Cheddar cheese.
- After 1 or 2 minutes, fold the omelet and cover the cheese. Cook another 1 to 2 minutes, until the cheese melts.
- Remove the omelet from the pan and serve.

Lunch

❧

Fudge Brownies

Nutritional Facts

Servings per container   9

Prep Total	10 min
Serving Size 2/3 cup (70g)	
Amount per serving	
Calories	10
	% Daily Value
Total Fat 20g	2%
Saturated Fat 2g	10%
Trans Fat 4g	-
Cholesterol	10%
Sodium 50mg	12%
Total Carbohydrate 7g	20%
Dietary Fiber 4g	7%
Total Sugar 12g	-
Protein 3g	
Vitamin C 2mcg	19%
Calcium 260mg	20%
Iron 8mg	8%
Potassium 235mg	6%

Ingredients

- 2 cups flour
- 2 cups sugar
- ½ cup of cocoa powder
- 1 teaspoon baking powder
- ½ teaspoon salt
- 1 cup vegetable oil
- 1 cup of water
- 1 teaspoon vanilla
- 1 cup dairy-free chocolate chips (optional)
- ½ cup chopped walnuts (optional)

Instructions:

- Preheat oven to 350°F and grease a 9 x 13-inch baking pan.
- Add dry ingredients in a mixing bowl. Whisk together wet ingredients and fold into the dry ingredients.
- If desired, add half the chocolate chips and chopped walnuts to the mix. Pour mixture into the prepared pan and sprinkle with remaining chocolate chips and walnuts, if using.
- For fudge-like brownies, bake for 20-25 minutes. For cake-like brownies, bake 25-30 minutes. Let the brownies cool slightly before serving.

POMEGRANATE QUINOA PORRIDGE

Nutritional Facts

Servings per container	4
Prep Total	10 min
Serving Size 2/3 cup (40g)	
Amount per serving	
Calories	22
	% Daily Value
Total Fat 12g	20%
Saturated Fat 2g	4%
Trans Fat 01g	1.22%
Cholesterol	22%
Sodium 170mg	10%
Total Carbohydrate 34g	22%
Dietary Fiber 5g	14%
Total Sugar 7g	-
Protein 3g	
Vitamin C 2mcg	10%
Calcium 260mg	20%

Iron 0mg	40%
Potassium 235mg	6%

Ingredients

- 1 1/2 cup quinoa flakes
- 2 1/2 teaspoons cinnamon
- 1 teaspoon vanilla extract
- 10 organic prunes, pitted and cut into 1/4's
- 1 pomegranate pulp
- 1/4 cup desiccated coconut
- Stewed apples
- Coconut flakes to garnish

Instructions:

- Gently place quinoa & almond milk into a saucepan, & stir on medium to low heat for 9 minutes, until it smooth
- Add cinnamon, desiccated coconut & vanilla extract & taste
- Pit prunes & cut into quarters, add to porridge and stir in well
- Serve in individual bowls
- Add a scoop of stewed apples (kindly view recipe below), pomegranates, prunes & coconut flakes
- Ready to eat!

Stewed apples

- Peel, core, slice apples and place into a saucepan with water
- Cook apples on medium heat, until extremely soft
- Remove from heat, drain & mash apples
- Ready to serve and enjoy your breakfast!

Sweet Corn Soup

Nutritional Facts

Servings per container	4
Prep Total	10 min
Serving Size 2/3 cup (50g)	
Amount per serving	
Calories	120
	% Daily Value
Total Fat 2g	5%
Saturated Fat 0g	8%
Trans Fat 2g	1.20%
Cholesterol	2%
Sodium 16mg	7%
Total Carbohydrate 7g	10%
Dietary Fiber 4g	10%
Total Sugar 12g	-
Protein 3g	
Vitamin C 2mcg	10%
Calcium 260mg	20%

Iron 20mg	25%
Potassium 235mg	8%

Ingredients

- 6 ears of corn
- 1 tablespoon corn oil
- 1 small onion
- 1/2 cup grated celery root
- 7 cups water or vegetable stock
- Add salt to taste

Instructions:

- Shuck the corn & slice off the kernels
- In a large soup pot put in the oil, onion, celery root, and one cup of water
- Let that mixture stew under low heat until the onion is soft
- Add the corn, salt & remaining water and bring it to a boil
- Cool briefly & then puree in a blender, then wait for it to cool before putting it through a food mill.
- Reheat & add salt with pepper to taste nice.

MEXICAN AVOCADO SALAD

Nutritional Facts

Servings per container	6
Prep Total	10 min
Serving Size 2/3 cup (70g)	
Amount per serving	
Calories	120
	% Daily Value
Total Fat 8g	10%
Saturated Fat 1g	8%
Trans Fat 0g	21
Cholesterol	22%
Sodium 16mg	7%
Total Carbohydrate 7g	13%
Dietary Fiber 4g	14%
Total Sugar 1g	-
Protein 2g	
Vitamin C 1mcg	1%
Calcium 260mg	20%

Iron 2mg	25%
Potassium 235mg	6%

Ingredients

- 24 cherry tomatoes, quartered
- 2 tablespoons extra-virgin olive oil
- 4 teaspoons red wine vinegar
- 2 teaspoon salt
- ¼ teaspoon freshly ground black pepper
- Gently chopped ½ medium yellow or white onion
- 1 jalapeño, seeded & finely chopped
- 2 tablespoons chopped fresh cilantro
- ¼ medium head iceberg lettuce, cut into ½-inch ribbons
- Chopped 2 ripe Hass avocados, seeded, peeled

Instructions:

- Add tomatoes, oil, vinegar, salt, & pepper in a neat medium bowl. Add onion, jalapeño & cilantro; toss well
- Put lettuce on a platter & top with avocado
- Spoon tomato mixture on top and serve.

CRAZY DELICIOUS RAW PAD THAI

Nutritional Facts

Servings per container	3
Prep Total	10 min
Serving Size 2/3 cup (77g)	
Amount per serving	
Calories	210
	% Daily Value
Total Fat 3g	10%
Saturated Fat 2g	8%
Trans Fat 7g	-
Cholesterol	0%
Sodium 120mg	7%
Total Carbohydrate 77g	10%
Dietary Fiber 4g	14%
Total Sugar 12g	-
Protein 3g	
Vitamin C 1mcg	20%
Calcium 260mg	20%

Iron 2mg	41%
Potassium 235mg	1%

Ingredients

- 2 large zucchini
- Thinly sliced ¼ red cabbage
- Chopped ¼ cup fresh mint leaves
- Sliced 1 spring onion
- Peeled and sliced ½ avocado
- 10 raw almonds
- 4 tablespoons sesame seeds Dressing
- ¼ cup peanut butter
- 2 tablespoons tahini
- 2 lemons, juiced
- 2 tablespoons tamari / salt-reduced soy sauce and add ½ chopped green chili

Instructions:

- Collect dressing ingredients in a container
- Pop the top on and shake truly well to mix. I like mine pleasant and smooth, however you can include a dash of filtered water if it looks excessively thick.
- Using a mandoline or vegetable peeler, remove one external portion of skin from every zucchini and dispose of.
- Combine zucchini strips, cabbage & dressing in a large mixing bowl and blend well
- Divide zucchini mix between two plates or bowls
- Top with residual fixings and enjoy it!

KALE AND WILD RICE STIR FLY

Nutritional Facts

Servings per container	3
Prep Total	10 min
Serving Size 2/3 cup (80g)	
Amount per serving	
Calories	220
	% Daily Value
Total Fat 5g	22%
Saturated Fat 1g	8%
Trans Fat 0g	-
Cholesterol	0%
Sodium 200mg	7%
Total Carbohydrate 12g	2%
Dietary Fiber 1g	14%
Total Sugar 12g	-
Protein 3g	
Vitamin C 2mcg	10%
Calcium 20mg	1%

Iron 2mg	2%
Potassium 235mg	6%

Ingredients

- 1 tablespoonful extra virgin olive oil
- Diced ¼ onion
- 3 carrots, cut into ½ inch slices
- 2 cups assorted mushrooms
- 2 bunch kale, chopped into bite-sized pieces
- 2 tablespoonful lemon juice
- 2 tablespoonful chili flakes, more if desired
- 1 tablespoon Braggs Liquid Aminos
- 2 cups wild rice, cooked

Instructions:

- In a large sauté pan, heat oil over on heater. Include onion & cook until translucent, for 35 to 10 minutes.
- Include carrots & sauté for another 2 minutes. Include mushrooms & cook for 4 minutes. Include kale, lemon juice, chili flakes & Braggs. Cook until kale is slightly wilted.
- Serve over wild rice and enjoy your Lunch!

Carpaccio

Nutrition Facts

- Calories: 350 kcal | Gross carbohydrates: 3 g | Protein: 31 g | Fat: 24 g | Fiber: 1 g | Net carbohydrates: 2 g | Macro fat: 42 % | Macro proteins: 54 % | Macro carbohydrates: 4 %

Total time: 5 minutes

Ingredients

- 100 grams of smoked prime rib
- 30 grams of arugula
- 20 grams of Parmesan cheese
- 10 grams of pine nuts
- 7 grams of butter
- 3 tablespoons olive oil with orange
- 1 tablespoon lemon juice
- pepper and salt

Instructions

- Arrange the meat slices on a plate.
- Wash the arugula and pat dry or use a salad spinner.
- Place the arugula on top of the meat.
- Scrape some curls from the Parmesan cheese and spread them over the arugula.
- Put the butter in a small frying pan. Add the pine nuts as soon as the butter has

melted. Let the pine nuts cook for a few minutes over medium heat and then sprinkle them over the carpaccio.

- Make the vinaigrette by mixing the lemon juice into the olive oil. Season with pepper and salt and drizzle over the carpaccio.

Keto spring frittata

Total time: 15 minutes

Nutrition Facts

- Calories: 955 kcal | Gross carbohydrates: 16 g | Protein: 46 g | Fats: 78 g | Fiber: 2 g | Net carbohydrates: 14 g | Macro fats: 57 % | Macro proteins: 33 % | Macro carbohydrates: 10 %

Ingredients

- 1 zucchini
- 0.5 bunch of mint
- 6 eggs
- Pinch of cayenne pepper
- 1 sprig of thyme or 1 teaspoon of dried thyme
- 80 grams of Pecorino cheese
- 0.5 red chili pepper
- 100 grams of feta cheese
- 3 tablespoons extra virgin olive oil
- 0.25 teaspoon truffle oil optional
- Salt to taste

Salad

- 50 grams of watercress
- 0.5 stalks of celery

- 75 grams of fresh (raw) peas still in the pod

- 1 tablespoon lemon juice

- 2 tablespoons extra virgin olive oil

- 200 grams of herb cheese or Boursin

Instructions

- Frittata:

- If you have an oven with a grill, turn the grill on at the highest setting.

- Grate the zucchini by hand or in the food processor and put it in a bowl. Sprinkle some salt over the grated zucchini.

- Put the zucchini in a strainer and press the zucchini firmly so that some of the moisture goes out.

- Wash the mint and pat dry. Remove the leaves from the twigs and cut them into pieces. Add to the zucchini and mix together.

- Heat the olive oil in a small (frying) pan over medium-high heat. Add the zucchini as soon as the oil is hot and spread over the pan. Lower the heat to moderate.

- Spread the zucchini over the pan

- Beat the eggs in the bowl and add the truffle oil, cayenne pepper and thyme leaves. Grate the pecorino and add half of the pecorino to the bowl.

- Beat eggs with thyme and cayenne pepper and truffle oil

- Pour the beaten eggs over the zucchini in the frying pan. Mix in the zucchini. Reduce the heat and simmer for 5 minutes while making the salad.

- Put the frittata in a baking dish or on a large plate and sprinkle the rest of the pecorino over it. Place as high as possible in the oven, just below the grill and brown for 5 minutes. If you don't have a grill, let the frittata cook on the stove for 5 minutes with a lid on the pan, if you want the cheese to melt you can gently turn the frittata by putting a lid or plate on the pan and then turning it over.

- Put frittata under the grill

- Wash the chili pepper and remove the seeds. Cut into small rings and sprinkle over the frittata as soon as it comes out of the oven. Also, crumble the feta over the frittata.

-

- Salad

- Bring a saucepan of water to the boil and add a pinch of salt.

- Wash the watercress and pat dry. Put it in a salad bowl. Wash the celery and cut it into 5 cm pieces and cut them into thin sticks (also use the celery leaves).

- Remove the peas from the cap and blanch them for 1-2 minutes in the boiling water in the saucepan (the same applies to frozen peas or snow peas). Then let them drain in a colander. If you have fresh peas from the pod this is not necessary.

- While the peas cool down, make a vinaigrette by mixing lemon juice with extra virgin olive oil.

- Add the peas to the salad and pour the vinaigrette over it. Mix everything together well.

Super-fast keto sandwiches

Nutrition Facts

- Calories: 112 kcal | Gross carbohydrates: 2 g | Protein: 9 g | Fats: 6 g | Fiber: 5 g | Net carbohydrates: -3 g | Macro fat: 50 % | Macro proteins: 75 % | Macro carbohydrates: -25 %

Total time: 10 minutes

Ingredients

- 1 teaspoon hemp flour
- 1 teaspoon almond flour
- 1 teaspoon of psyllium
- 1 teaspoon baking powder
- 1 egg at room temperature
- 1 teaspoon extra virgin olive oil or melted butter

Instructions

- Put the dry ingredients in a cup and mix well. In particular, ensure that the baking powder is no longer visible. It helps if you put the baking powder through a (tea) strainer.
- Now add the egg and the butter. The egg must be at room temperature. If it is not, then place it for about 10 minutes in a bowl with hot tap water.

- Stir well and let it stand for a while. You will see that there are some bubbles in the batter.

- Now put the cup in the microwave for 1 minute on the highest setting. When you take the cup out, you want the top of the batter to be dry. If it is still wet, then put it in the microwave for a little longer. (If you put several cups in the microwave at the same time, you may have to extend the time slightly depending on your type of microwave).

- Once the top is dry, remove the cup from the microwave and turn it on a cutting board. Decide now if you want thick rolls or something thinner. So, cut into 2 or 3 or 4 slices. Keep in mind that these slices must fit in your toaster.

- Now toast the bread slices in your toaster until they are firm but not hard.

- Your bread is now ready. You can use it immediately or use it for your breakfast or lunch the next day. Spread it well with butter so that you get enough fats.

Keto Croque Monsieur

Total time: 7 minutes

Ingredients

- 2 eggs
- 25 grams of grated cheese
- 25 grams of ham 1 large slice
- 40 ml of cream
- 40 ml mascarpone
- 30 grams of butter
- Pepper and salt
- Basil leaves optional, to garnish

Instructions

- Beat the eggs in a bowl, add some salt and pepper.
- Add the cream, mascarpone and grated cheese and stir together.
- Melt the butter over medium heat. The butter must not turn brown. Once the butter has melted, set the heat to low.
- Add half of the omelet mixture to the frying pan and then immediately place the slice of ham on it. Now pour the rest of the omelet mixture over the ham and then immediately put a lid on it.
- Allow 2-3 minutes of fry over low heat until the top is slightly firmer.

- Slide the omelet onto the lid to turn the omelet. Then put the omelet back in the frying pan to fry for another 1-2 minutes on the other side (still on low heat), then put the lid back on the pan.
- Don't let the omelet cook for too long! It does not matter if it is still liquid. Garnish with a few basil leaves if necessary.

Keto wraps with cream cheese and salmon

Nutrition Facts

- Calories: 479 kcal | Gross carbohydrates: 4 g | Protein: 16 g | Fats: 45 g | Net carbohydrates: 4 g | Macro fats: 69 % | Macro proteins: 25 % | Macro carbohydrates: 6 %

Total time: 10 minutes

Ingredients

- 80 grams of cream cheese
- 1 tablespoon dill or other fresh herbs
- 30 grams of smoked salmon
- 1 egg
- 15 grams of butter
- Pinch of cayenne pepper
- Pepper and salt

Instructions

- Beat the egg well in a bowl. With 1 egg you can make two thin wraps in a small frying pan.
- Melt the butter over medium heat in a small frying pan. Once the butter has melted, add half of the beaten egg to the pan. Move the pan back and forth so that the entire

bottom is covered with a very thin layer of egg. Turn down the heat!

- Carefully loosen the egg on the edges with a silicone spatula and turn the wafer-thin omelet as soon as the egg is no longer dripping (about 45 seconds to 1 minute). You can do this by sliding it onto a lid or plate and then sliding it back into the pan. Let the other side be cooked in about 30 seconds and then remove from the pan. The omelet must be nice and light yellow. Repeat for the rest of the beaten egg.

- Once the omelets are ready, let them cool on a cutting board or plate and make the filling.

- Cut the dill into small pieces and put it in a bowl.

- Add the cream cheese and the salmon, cut them into small pieces. Mix together. Add a tiny bit of cayenne pepper and mix well. Taste for a moment and then season with salt and pepper.

- Spread a layer on the wrap and roll it up. Cut the wrap in half and keep in the fridge until you eat it.

Savory keto broccoli cheese muffins

Nutrition Facts

- Calories: 349 kcal | Gross carbohydrates: 4 g | Protein: 28 g | Fats: 25 g | Fiber: 1 g | Net carbohydrates: 3 g | Macro fat: 45 % | Macro proteins: 50 % | Macro carbohydrates: 5 %

Preparation time: 10 minutes

Ingredients

- 4 eggs
- 75 grams of Parmesan cheese
- 125 grams of fresh cheese
- 125 grams of mozzarella
- 75 grams of broccoli
- 1.5 teaspoon baking powder
- 0.25 teaspoon garlic powder
- 0.25 teaspoon mustard

Instructions

- Preheat the oven to 160 ° Celsius.
- Cut the broccoli into small pieces. Bring a saucepan with water to the boil and as soon as the water boils, add the broccoli pieces to the pan. Blanch the broccoli for 1 minute in the boiling water.
- Drain the broccoli well in a colander.

- Grate the Parmesan cheese and the fresh cheese. Cut the mozzarella into small pieces.

- Beat the eggs well in a bowl.

- Add the cheese, broccoli and mustard to the eggs. Mix well together.

- Then add the garlic powder and baking powder and stir well again.

- Add garlic powder and baking powder

- Preferably fill a silicone muffin tray with the broccoli-cheese egg batter and bake for 10 minutes. You can also use paper muffin cases, but they are difficult to remove.

- Bake the muffins in the preheated oven until done.

- If you put a skewer in the middle of a muffin, it must come out clean (without batter). Then your muffins are ready.

- Check if the muffin is cooked with a satay skewer.

Keto rusk

Nutrition Facts

- Calories: 53 kcal | Gross carbohydrates: 1 g | Protein: 2 g | Fats: 4 g | Fiber: 0 g | Net carbohydrates: 1 g | Macro fats: 57 % | Macro proteins: 29 % | Macro carbohydrates: 14 %

Time: 9 minutes

Ingredients

- 35 grams of almond flour
- 1 egg
- 1 tablespoon butter
- 0.5 teaspoon baking powder
- 1/8 teaspoon of salt

Instructions

- Preheat the oven to 200° Celsius.
- Put all the ingredients in a cup and mix them well together with a fork. You want a narrower, higher cup that can go into the microwave.
- Put the cup on the highest position of the microwave for 90 seconds.
- Allow the dough to cool for a few minutes and then place it on a cutting board.
- Cut the dough into 5 equal slices and place them on a sheet of baking paper on the baking sheet.
- Bake for 5-6 minutes until golden and crispy.

Flax seed hemp flour bun

Total time: 8 minutes

Nutrition Facts

- Calories: 182kcal | Gross carbohydrates: 5 g | Protein: 11g | Fats: 15g Fiber: 12 g | Net carbohydrates: -7g | Macro fats: 79% | Macro proteins: 58% | Macro carbohydrates: -37%

Ingredients

- 1 teaspoon hemp flour
- 1 teaspoon linseed flour
- 1 teaspoon of psyllium
- 1 teaspoon baking powder
- 1 egg at room temperature
- 0.5 teaspoon butter or mild olive oil or ghee

Instructions

- Preheat the oven to 180 ° C (hot air oven) if you want to bake in the oven, otherwise use a toaster.
- Put all dry ingredients in a large cup or bowl that can be put in the microwave. Mix everything together. Make sure that you no longer see the baking powder (so no white lumps) or put the baking powder through a sieve.

- Add the egg and the butter (melted but not necessary) and mix well. Put in the microwave on the highest setting for 1 minute. The dark bun in the photo is this bun.
- Remove the sandwich from the cup and halve or cut it into three slices. Bake those slices for 5 minutes in the preheated oven or bake them in a toaster.

Keto muffins with Roquefort

Nutrition Facts

- Calories: 160kcal | Gross carbohydrates: 2g | Protein: 6g | Fats: 14g Fiber: 1g | Net carbohydrates: 1 g | Macro fats: 67% | Macro proteins: 29% | Macro carbohydrates: 5%

Total time: 18 minutes

Ingredients

- 150 grams of zucchini
- 50 ml extra virgin olive oil
- Pepper to taste
- 100 grams of red pepper
- 75 grams of Roquefort
- 100 grams of mascarpone
- 6 eggs
- 1.5 teaspoon baking powder

Instructions

- Preheat the oven to 175 ° Celsius.
- Wash the zucchini and bell pepper and pat dry. Remove the seeds from the bell pepper and cut the bell pepper and zucchini into small cubes.

- Heat the olive oil in a frying pan over medium-high heat and fry the zucchini and bell pepper in about 5 minutes to soften.

- Beat the eggs with the baking powder. You don't want any lumps of baking powder, so you must either beat very well or put the baking powder through a tea strainer first.

- Mix the vegetables, the batter, mascarpone and cheese together and then divide over the muffin tins.

- Bake for 15 minutes in the preheated oven. Check with a satay skewer if they are done. If you put the stick in the middle of a muffin it must come out dry. If you still have batter, you have to let the muffins bake a little longer.

Keto wrap

Nutrition Facts

- Calories: 128 kcal | Gross carbohydrates: 1 g | Protein: 6g | Fats: 12g Fiber: 0.3 g | Net carbohydrates: 1 g | Macro fats: 64% | Macro proteins: 32% | Macro carbohydrates: 4%

Total time: 5 minutes

Ingredients

- 1 egg
- 0.5 teaspoon coconut oil or mild olive oil or butter
- 0.5 teaspoon curry powder or other herbs or spices

Instructions

- Heat the coconut fat (or mild olive oil or butter) in a small frying pan over high heat.
- Put the egg in a bowl and add the curry powder and some salt. Beat it well with a fork or whisk.
- Turn down the heat now. Pour the batter into the frying pan and tilt the pan a little so that the batter runs out and covers the entire bottom of the pan.
- Bake this wafer-thin omelet in 10-20 seconds. Carefully remove (with a trowel) the edges of the wrap from the sides of the pan.

- Turn the wrap over and bake for a few seconds on the other side. As soon as the edges start to curl up, remove it from the pan (this is very fast!).

Notes

If you make several wraps you only have to put some oil in the pan the first time.

Dinner

Creamy Avocado Pasta

Nutritional Facts

Servings per container	7
Prep Total	10 min
Serving Size 2/3 cup (25g)	
Amount per serving	
Calories	19
	% Daily Value
Total Fat 8g	300%
Saturated Fat 1g	40%
Trans Fat 0g	20%
Cholesterol	6%
Sodium 210mg	3%
Total Carbohydrate 22g	400%
Dietary Fiber 4g	1%

Total Sugar 12g	02.20%
Protein 3g	
Vitamin C 2mcg	20%
Calcium 10mg	6%
Iron 4mg	7%
Potassium 25mg	6%

Ingredients

- 340 g / 12 oz. spaghetti
- 2 ripe avocados, halved, seeded & neatly peeled
- 1/2 cup fresh basil leaves
- 3 cloves garlic
- 1/3 cup olive oil
- 2-3 Teaspoons freshly squeezed lemon juice
- Add sea salt & black pepper, to taste
- 1.5 cups cherry tomatoes, halved

Instructions:

1. In a large pot of boiling salted water, cook pasta according to the package. When al dente, drain and set aside.
2. To make the avocado sauce, combine avocados, basil, garlic, oil, and lemon juice in the food processor. Blend on high until smooth. Season with salt and pepper to taste.
3. In a large bowl, combine pasta, avocado sauce, and cherry tomatoes until evenly coated.
4. To serve, top with additional cherry tomatoes, fresh basil, or lemon zest.
5. Best when fresh. Avocado will oxidize over time so store leftovers in a covered container in refrigerator up to one day.

BLACK BEAN VEGAN WRAPS

Nutritional Facts

Servings per container	5
Prep Total	10 min
Serving Size 2/3 cup (27g)	
Amount per serving	
Calories	200
	% Daily Value
Total Fat 8g	1%
Saturated Fat 1g	2%
Trans Fat 0g	2%
Cholesterol	2%
Sodium 240mg	7%
Total Carbohydrate 12g	2%
Dietary Fiber 4g	14%
Total Sugar 12g	01.21%
Protein 3g	
Vitamin C 2mcg	2%
Calcium 20mg	1%

Iron 7mg	2%
Potassium 25mg	6%

Ingredients

- 1 1/2 half cups of beans (sprouted & cooked)
- 2 carrots
- 1 or 2 tomatoes
- 2 avocadoes
- 1 cob of corn
- 1 Kale
- 2 or 3 sticks of celery
- 2 persimmons
- 1 Coriander

Dressing:

- 1 Hachiya Persimmon (or half a mango)
- Juice of 1 lemon
- 2 to 3 tablespoons original olive oil
- 1/4 clean cup water
- 1 or 2 teaspoons grated fresh ginger
- 1/2 teaspoon of salt

Instructions:

- Sprout & cook the black beans
- Chop all the ingredients & mix them in a neat bowl with the black beans
- Mix all the ingredients for the dressing & pour into the salad
- Serve a spoonful in a clean lettuce leaf that you can easily roll into a wrap. Most people use iceberg or romaine lettuce.

ZUCCHINI PASTA WITH PESTO SAUCE

Nutritional Facts

Servings per container	5
Prep Total	10 min
Serving Size 2/3 cup (20g)	
Amount per serving	
Calories	100
	% Daily Value
Total Fat 8g	12%
Saturated Fat 1g	2%
Trans Fat 0g	20%
Cholesterol	2%
Sodium 10mg	7%
Total Carbohydrate 7g	2%
Dietary Fiber 2g	14%
Total Sugar 1g	01.20%
Protein 3g	
Vitamin C 2mcg	10%

Calcium 240mg	1%
Iron 2mg	2%
Potassium 25mg	6%

Ingredients

- 1 to 2 medium zucchinis (make noodles with a mandoline or spiralizer)
- 1/2 teaspoon of salt

For Pesto

- Soaked 1/4 cup cashews
- Soaked 1/4 cup pine nuts
- 1/2 cup spinach
- 1/2 cup peas you can make it fresh or frozen one
- 1/4 cup broccoli
- 1/4 cup basil leaves
- 1/2 avocado
- 1 or 2 tablespoons original olive oil
- 2 tablespoons nutritional yeast
- 1/2 teaspoon salt
- Pinch black-pepper

Instructions:

- Place zucchini noodles in a strainer over a clean bowl
- Include 1/2 teaspoon of salt & let it set while preparing the pesto sauce
- Mix all the ingredients for the pesto sauce
- Extract excess water from zucchini noodles & place them in a clean bowl
- Pour the sauce on top & garnish with some basil leaves & pine nuts

BALSAMIC BBQ SEITAN AND TEMPEH RIBS

Nutritional Facts

Servings per container	4
Prep Total	10 min
Serving Size 2/3 cup (56g)	
Amount per serving	
Calories	100
	% Daily Value
Total Fat 7g	1%
Saturated Fat 1g	2%
Trans Fat 0g	20%
Cholesterol	2%
Sodium 160mg	7%
Total Carbohydrate 37g	2%
Dietary Fiber 2g	1%
Total Sugar 2g	01.20%
Protein 14g	
Vitamin C 1mcg	10%

Calcium 450mg	1%
Iron 2mg	2%
Potassium 35mg	7%

Ingredients

For the spice rub

- 1/4 cup raw turbinado sugar
- 1 or 2 tablespoons this should be smoked paprika
- 1 tablespoon cayenne pepper
- Minced 3 garlic cloves
- 2 tablespoons dried oregano
- 2 tablespoons Kosher salt
- 2 ½ tablespoons ground black pepper
- Minced ¼ cup fresh parsley

Instructions:

- In a clean bowl, mix the ingredients for the spice rub. Blend well & put aside.

- In a small saucepan over medium heat, combine the apple juice vinegar, balsamic vinegar, maple syrup, ketchup, red onion, garlic, and chile. Mix & let stew sit, exposed, for around 60 minutes. Increase the level of the heat to medium-high & cook for 15 additional minutes until the sauce thickens. Mix it frequently. If it appears to be excessively thick, include some water.

- Preheat the oven to 350 degrees. In a clean bowl, mix the dry ingredients for the seitan & blend well. In a clean bowl, add the wet ingredients. Add the wet ingredients to the dry & blend until simply consolidated. Manipulate the dough gently until everything is combined & the dough feels elastic.

- Grease or shower a preparing dish. Include the dough to the baking dish, smoothing it & stretching it to fit the dish. Cut the dough into 7 to 9 strips & afterward down the middle to make 16 thick ribs.

- Top the dough with the flavor rub & back rub it in a bit. Heat the seitan for

40 minutes to an hour or until the seitan has a strong surface to it. Remove the dish from the heater. Recut the strips & cautiously remove them from the baking dish.

- Increase the oven temperature to about 400 degrees. Slather the ribs with BBQ sauce & lay them on a baking sheet. Set the ribs back in the heater for about 12 minutes so the sauce can get a bit roasted. Then again, you can cook the sauce-covered ribs on a grill or in a grill pan.

GREEN BEAN CASSEROLE

Nutritional Facts

Servings per container	**2**
Prep Total	10 min
Serving Size 2/3 cup (5g)	
Amount per serving	
Calories	100
	% Daily Value
Total Fat 10g	12%
Saturated Fat 2g	2%
Trans Fat 4g	20%
Cholesterol	2%
Sodium 70mg	7%
Total Carbohydrate 18g	2%
Dietary Fiber 9g	10%
Total Sugar 16g	01.20%
Protein 2g	
Vitamin C 9mcg	10%

Calcium 720mg	1%
Iron 6mg	2%
Potassium 150mg	6%

Ingredients

- Diced 1 large onion
- 3 tablespoons of original olive oil
- ¼ cup flour
- 2 cups of water
- 1 tablespoons of salt
- ½ tablespoons of garlic powder
- 1 or 2 bags frozen green beans (10 ounces each)
- 1 fried onion

Instructions:

- Preheat oven to 350 degrees.
- Heat original olive oil in a shallow pan. Include onion & stir occasionally while the onions soften and turn translucent. This takes about 15 to 20 minutes, don't rush it because it gives so much flavor! Once the onion is well cooked, include flour & stir well to cook the flour. It will be a dry mixture. Include salt & garlic powder. Add some water. Let simmer for about 1 – 2 minutes & allow the mixture to thicken. Immediately remove from heat.
- Pour green beans into a square baking dish & add 2/3 can of onions. Include all of the gravy & stir well to together.
- Place in oven & cook for 25 to 30 minutes, gravy mixture will be bubbly. Top with remaining fried onions & cook for 4 to 12 minutes more. Serve immediately and enjoy your dinner.

SOCCA PIZZA [VEGAN]

Nutritional Facts

Servings per container 2

Prep Total	10 min
Serving Size 2/3 cup (78g)	
Amount per serving	
Calories	120
	% Daily Value
Total Fat 10g	20%
Saturated Fat 5g	7%
Trans Fat 6g	27%
Cholesterol	5%
Sodium 10mg	10%
Total Carbohydrate 4g	20%
Dietary Fiber 9g	15%
Total Sugar 12g	01.70%
Protein 6g	
Vitamin C 7mcg	10%

Calcium 290mg	20%
Iron 4mg	2%
Potassium 240mg	7%

Ingredients

Socca Base

- 1 cup chickpea (garbanzo bean) flour – I used-Bob's Red Mill Garbanzo Fava Flour
- 1 or 2 cups of cold, filtered water
- 1 to 2 tablespoons of minced garlic
- ½ tablespoon of sea salt
- 2 tablespoons of coconut oil (for greasing)

Toppings

- Add Tomato-paste
- Add Dried Italian herbs (oregano, basil, thyme, rosemary, etc.)
- Add Mushrooms
- Add Red onion
- Add Capsicum/bell pepper
- Add Sun-dried tomatoes
- Add Kalamata olives
- Add Vegan Cheese & Chopped Fresh basil leaves

Instructions:

- Pre-heat oven to 350F.
- In a clean mixing bowl, whisk together garbanzo bean flour & water until there are no lumps remaining. Stir together in garlic and sea salt. Allow to rest for about 12 minutes to thicken.
- Grease 2 - 4 small, shallow dishes/tins with original coconut oil.
- Pour mixture into a clean dish & bake for about 20 - 15 minutes or until golden brown.

- Remove dishes from the oven, top with your favorite toppings & vegan cheese (optional) & return to the oven for another 7 - 10 minutes or so.
- Remove dishes from oven & allow to sit for about 2 – 5 minutes before removing pizzas from the dishes. Enjoy your dinner!

Mediterranean salad with quinoa and rocket

Nutrition Facts

Time: 20 min

- kcal: 401
- KH: 23 g
- E: 6 g
- Q: 30 g

Ingredients

- 40 grams of quinoa
- 1 lime freshly pressed
- 60 g paprika, green, fresh
- 60 g small cucumber
- 1 tomato / n
- 1 small onion, red
- 50 g olives black raw
- 50g rocket, fresh
- 2 stems of basil fresh
- 1 small parsnip raw
- 4 tablespoons olive oil
- 1 pinch of sea salt (Fleur de sell)
- 1 pinch of pepper, black

Preparation

- Put the quinoa in a sieve and rinse with running water to remove any bitter substances.
- Cover the quinoa in a saucepan with water and simmer for 8 - 10 minutes, then drain and leave the granules in the pan.
- Season the quinoa with lime juice, salt and pepper.
- Remove paprika from kernels and dividers and cut them into small pieces
- Peel the cucumber and cut it into small pieces
- Cut tomato into small pieces
- Peel the onion and cut it into thin rings.
- Peel and slice the parsnip
- Wash the rucola leaves and drain well, remove them for too long ends
- Wash the basil and shake dry, then peel off the leaves.
- Mix the quinoa, paprika, cucumber, tomato, onion, parsnip, rocket and olives in a bowl
- Add the olive oil and season with salt and pepper.
- Put the salad on two plates and sprinkle with basil leaves.

Baked chicken thighs in lemon sage butter

Nutrition Facts

Time: 50 min

- kcal: 793
- KH: 5 g
- E: 48g
- F: 63 g

Ingredients

- 3 chicken thighs, with skin and bones
- 2 lemon / n
- 10 stems of thyme fresh
- 2 stems of rosemary fresh
- 2 stems of sage fresh
- 100 g of butter
- 2 tbsp. olive oil
- 1 teaspoon sea salt (Fleur de sel)
- 1 pinch of pepper, black
- 10 garlic toes

Preparation

- Separate chicken thighs, i.e. loosen the thighs from the lower leg
- Season with salt and pepper
- Wash the herbs and shake dry
- Crush the garlic cloves unpeeled with the flat side of the knife.
- Wash and slice the lemons
- Heat the olive oil in the pan and add the meat with herbs, lemons and garlic.
- Fry the meat all around, then place in the pan for 30 minutes at 175 ° C in the preheated oven.
- Then remove the pan from the oven and take out the pieces of meat.
- Put the butter in the pan and bring to a boil.
- Put the meat back into the pan and drizzle the butter with the spoon several times over the meat.
- Serve the chicken hot in the pan

Zucchini pasta with pesto

Nutrition Facts

2Time: 20 min

- kcal: 449
- KH: 12 g
- E: 16g
- F: 35 g

Ingredients

- 500 g of zucchini
- 50 g paprika, yellow, fresh
- 30 g of cashew nuts
- 40 g Ricotta Magerstufe
- 30 g of Parmesan
- 1 tsp. turmeric, powder
- 1 pinch of sea salt (Fleur de sel)
- 1 pinch of pepper, black
- 50 g of olive oil

Preparation

- Wash the peppers, remove the cores and partitions and cut into wide strips.

- Place the strips of paprika on a baking sheet with the skin side up and roast under the grill for 8 - 10 minutes at 200 ° C until the skin throws bubbles.

- Then remove the tin, cover the pepper strips with a damp dishcloth and allow to cool slightly.

- Carefully remove the skin.

- Roast the cashews in a frying pan until golden brown, in between panning several times

- Put the cashews, paprika, ricotta, coarsely grated Parmesan, turmeric, salt, pepper and olive oil in a shaker and puree with the hand blender.

- Wash and dry the zucchini, then cut off the ends and make long zucchini noodles with the spiral cutter.

- Blanch the zucchini noodles in a pot of boiling salted water for a few minutes, then drain off the water.

- Add the pesto to the noodles and mix. Finally, season with salt and pepper again.

- Fill the zucchini noodles on two plates and sprinkle with freshly squeezed lemon juice.

Roasted pork steak with vegetables

Nutrition Facts

Time: 20 min

- kcal: 714
- KH: 12 g
- E: 58 g
- F: 48 g

Ingredients

- 250 g pork chop, boneless
- 100 g zucchini, raw
- 40 g paprika, red, fresh
- 40 g paprika, yellow, fresh
- 40 g paprika, green, fresh
- 50 g mushrooms, brown
- 5 stems of thyme, fresh
- 2 tbsp. olive oil
- 1 tbsp. butter
- 1 pinch of sea salt (Fleur de sel)
- 1 pinch of pepper, black

Preparation

- Wash vegetables and drain
- Slice zucchini at an angle
- Cut peppers into strips
- Clean and halve mushrooms
- Wash thyme and shake dry.
- Put the pork chop in the hot grill pan, add the thyme and grill the meat from both sides.
- Heat butter and oil in the second pan and fry the zucchini, peppers and mushrooms.
- Season the vegetables with salt and pepper and place them on a plate
- Season the pork chop and add to the vegetables.

Salmon in cream sauce with peas and lemon

Nutrition Facts

Time: 25 min

- kcal: 1024
- KH: 19 g
- E: 61 g
- Q: 78 g

Ingredients

- 500 g salmon filet, without skin
- 150 g peas green raw
- 200 ml whipped cream 30%
- 2 small shallots / n
- 1 toe garlic
- 20 g of Parmesan
- 40 g of butter
- 1 lemon / n medium
- 1 pinch of nutmeg
- 1 pinch of pepper, white
- 1 pinch of sea salt

Preparation

- Wash the salmon and pat dry, then cut them into bite-sized pieces.
- Peel the shallots and finely dice.
- Peel the garlic and finely chop.
- Heat the butter in the pan, add shallots and garlic and fry the salmon pieces in it.
- Add the cream and stir.
- Add the peas and simmer briefly over medium heat.
- Meanwhile, wash the lemon hot, dry and rub the bowl with the grater.
- Halve the lemon and squeeze out the juice.
- Add grated Parmesan, lemon peel and a little nutmeg to the pan and stir.
- Season with lemon juice, salt and pepper.

Steamed vegetable pan

Nutrition Facts

Time: 10 min

- kcal: 239
- KH: 27 g
- E: 9 g
- F: 10g

Ingredients

- 100 g of broccoli

- 50 g paprika, red, fresh

- 50 g paprika, yellow, fresh

- 50 g onion

- 100 g Kaiserschoten, fresh

- 2 medium carrots

- 1 pinch of sea salt (Fleur de sel)

- 1 tbsp. olive oil

Preparation

- Wash the broccoli and cut the florets from the stalk

- Remove the peppers from the seeds and partitions and cut them into strips.

- Peel the onion and cut it into rings

- Wash and drain the pears

- Peel the carrot and cut it into thin sticks.

- Heat the olive oil in the pan

- Put the prepared vegetables in the pan and fry them all over, stirring several times.

- Season everything with salt and serve.

Chicken breast with pan vegetables

Nutrition Facts

Time: 30 min

- kcal: 382
- KH: 17 g
- E: 48g
- Q: 11 g

Ingredients

- 180 g chicken breast, without skin
- 80 g Brussels sprouts
- 120 g carrot
- 120 g onion
- 1 pinch of sea salt (Fleur de sel)
- 1 pinch of pepper, black
- 1 tbsp. olive oil
- 1 stalk of parsley, fresh

Preparation

- Wash chicken breast and pat dry
- Remove the dry stem and withered leaves from the sprouts, then halve each time.

- Peel carrot and slice

- Peel onion and cut it into pieces

- Wash parsley and shake dry, then chop.

- Heat the olive oil in the pan and fry the chicken breast from both sides until golden brown until the meat is cooked.

- Season the chicken breast with salt and pepper.

- Add the vegetables to the hot pan and fry, then season with salt and pepper.

- Place the chicken breast with the pan vegetables on a plate and sprinkle with Petersilia.

Frittata with spinach and grainy cream cheese

Nutrition Facts

Time: 40 min

- kcal: 399
- KH: 3 g
- E: 28g
- Q: 30 g

Ingredients

- 4,00 eggs size M
- 30 g spinach, raw
- 3 tablespoons whipped cream 30%
- 50 g of Parmesan
- 100 g granular cream cheese, 20% fat i.Tr
- 1 pinch of sea salt (Fleur de sel)
- 1 pinch of pepper, black
- 1 tbsp. olive oil

Preparation

- Wash the spinach and drain well.
- Beat the eggs and stir in a bowl with whipped cream.

- Add the cream cheese and season with salt and pepper.

- Stir again.

- Heat the olive oil in the pan and add the egg mass.

- Add the spinach leaves and let the egg mass stagnate over medium heat.

- Then add freshly grated Parmesan cheese over the egg mass.

- Place the frittata in the pan for 15 - 20 minutes in the oven preheated to 180 ° C.

- Remove the finished frittata from the oven and cut it into pieces, drizzle with freshly squeezed lemon juice and serve.

Mushroom pan with cream sauce and herbs

Nutrition Facts

Time: 15 min

- kcal: 431
- KH: 11 g
- E: 10g
- Q: 39 g

Ingredients

- 250 g mushrooms, brown
- 100 g whipped cream 30%
- 10 g butter
- 2 toes of garlic
- 1 pinch of sea salt (Fleur de sel)
- 1 pinch of pepper, black
- 1 pinch of nutmeg
- 1 shallot / n
- 1 stalk of oregano, fresh

Preparation

- Brush the mushrooms, brush with a brush if necessary, then cut off the dry ends of the stems

- Slice the mushrooms
- Peel the garlic and cut it into thin slices.
- Peel the shallot and dice finely.
- Heat the butter in the pan and sauté the shallot with garlic.
- Add mushrooms and fry everything for a few minutes.
- Add the cream and season everything with salt, pepper and fresh grated nutmeg.
- Wash the oregano and shake it dry.
- Serve the mushroom frying pan with cream sauce and herbs.

False bulgur salad with paprika and fresh mint

Nutrition Facts

Time: 30 min

- kcal: 148
- KH: 9 g
- E: 3 g
- F: 10g

Ingredients

- 300 g of cauliflower
- 80 g paprika, red, fresh
- 80 g paprika, yellow, fresh
- 80 g pepper, green, fresh
- 2 small tomatoes / n
- 1 small onion, red
- 2 cloves of garlic
- 2 spring onions / n
- 5 stems of coriander, fresh
- 1 lemon / s freshly pressed
- 4 tablespoons olive oil
- 1 pinch of sea salt (Fleur de sel)

- 1 pinch of pepper, black
- 1 pinch cumin dried
- 2 stalks of mint

Preparation

- Wash the cauliflower, place in a pot with steaming insert and blanch for a few minutes, it should not be too soft.
- Grind cauliflower with the grater.
- Wash and drain the remaining vegetables and herbs.
- Cut the peppers into small cubes.
- Quarter the tomatoes, remove the stalk and cut it into pieces.
- Peel the onion and cut it into thin rings.
- Cut the spring onions into rings.
- Pick the leaves of coriander and mint from the stalk and chop them roughly.
- Place all prepared ingredients in a salad bowl.
- Add olive oil, a little lemon juice, cumin, salt and pepper to the salad and mix.
- Season the salad and chill until it is consumed.

For a better taste, the salad should have some time to sit.

Dessert & snacks + Extra Everyday Recipes

Fried sea bream with fresh mango salsa

Nutritional Facts

Time: 30 min

- kcal: 326
- KH: 15 g
- E: 37 g
- F: 13 g

Ingredients

- 4 small bream, fillet
- 100 g mango, raw
- 100 g cucumber with peel, raw
- 100 g paprika, red, fresh
- 50 g spinach, raw
- 30 g of Parmesan, grated
- 1 pinch of sea salt (Fleur de sel)
- 1 pinch of pepper, black
- 1 g lemon / n

- 1 tbsp. olive oil

Preparation

- Wash bream and pat dry
- Peel the mango and cut the pulp into small slices
- Wash the cucumber and cut it into small pieces
- Remove the peppers from the seeds and partitions and cut it into small cubes.
- Wash the spinach and dry it in the salad spinner
- Remove too long stalks from the spinach
- Wash and dry the lemon, then make lemon zest with the grater
- Halve the lemon and squeeze out the juice.
- Mix mango, cucumber, paprika and a little lemon juice in a bowl and season with salt and pepper.
- Put spinach leaves on two plates.
- Heat the olive oil in the frying pan and fry the bream fillets on both sides .
- Season the fillets with salt and pepper and sprinkle with freshly grated Parmesan.
- Add the fish fillets to the spinach and serve together with the mango salsa.

Vital red cabbage salad with nuts and seeds

Nutritional Facts

Time: 10 min

- kcal: 206
- KH: 19 g
- E: 6 g
- F: 13 g

Ingredients

- 150 g red cabbage, raw
- 20 g walnut kernels, fresh
- 1 tbsp. balsamic vinegar (balsamic vinegar)
- 1 teaspoon agave syrup
- 1 pinch of sea salt (Fleur de sel)
- 1 pinch of pepper, black
- 5 g of chard, raw

Preparation

- For red cabbage, remove the outer leaves, then quarter with a knife, remove the stalk and cut it into very fine strips with the knife. Or plane with the vegetable slicer in very fine strips.

- Add the balsamic, agave syrup, salt and pepper to the bowl and mix. Rinse chard and dry.

- Put the red cabbage and chard in the bowl and mix with the dressing. Finely chop walnut kernels.

- Arrange red cabbage salad on a plate or in a bowl and serve with the chopped walnut kernels.

Omelet with eggplant and tomato

Nutritional Facts

Time: 20 min

- kcal: 416
- KH: 8 g
- E: 29 g
- Q: 29 g

Ingredients

- 4 size M egg, from chicken, raw
- 100 g cherry tomatoes
- 50 g aubergine, raw
- 1 stalk of basil, fresh
- 1 tbsp whipped cream 30%
- 1 pinch of sea salt (Fleur de sel)
- 1 pinch of pepper, black
- 1 tsp. olive oil

Preparation

- Wash aubergine and tomatoes, drain and slice.
- Lightly salt eggplant.

- Beat the eggs in a bowl and whisk with cream, a little salt and pepper.

- Heat the oil in the pan and add the egg mass.

- Spread the aubergines and tomato slices on top.

- Put the lid on the pan and let everything fade.

- Season with salt and pepper and sprinkle with basil.

- Carefully fold the omelet in half and place it on a plate.

Chickpea salad with halloumi

Nutritional Facts

Time: 20 min

- kcal: 662
- KH: 27 g
- E: 29 g
- F: 46 g

Ingredients

- 200 g of chickpeas
- 200 g Halloumi
- 1 shallot
- ½ spring onion / n
- 30 g of radish raw
- 50 g tomato / n
- 50 g of cucumber
- 20 g of sweetcorn canned
- 4 stems of parsley
- 4 tablespoons olive oil
- 1 pinch of sea salt
- 1 pinch of pepper, black

Preparation

- Chickpeas in a colander and rinse under running water, then drain
- Heat pan and fry Halloumi from both sides until roast strips are recognizable
- Halloumi with salt and pepper, then remove from the pan and cut into pieces.
- Meanwhile, clean the radishes and cut into thin slices.
- Wash tomatoes and cut into pieces.
- Remove the peppers from the seeds and partitions and cut into pieces.
- Wash the cucumber and cut into small cubes.
- Peel the shallot and cut it into fine rings
- Clean the spring onion and cut into rings at an angle.
- Wash the parsley and shake it dry, then pluck the leaves and chop them.
- Remove the corn from the tin and drain.
- Put all the prepared salad ingredients in a bowl and mix.
- Add olive oil and some salt and pepper and stir again.
- Put the chickpeas salad with halloumi on two plates and serve.

Salad with chard, avocado, nuts and feta

Nutritional Facts

Time: 10 min

- kcal: 447
- KH: 10 g
- E: 14 g
- Q: 39 g

Ingredients

- 20 g of chard
- 60 g avocado, hate, fresh
- 50 g of tomatoes dried
- 30 g of feta
- 30 g walnut kernels, fresh
- 20 g onion, red
- 1 pinch of sea salt
- 1 pinch of pepper, black

Preparation

- Wash the chard and drain well
- Halve the avocado and remove the kernel, then peel the pulp and cut into small

pieces.

- Cut the dried tomatoes into pieces.
- Crumble feta by hand.
- Chop walnuts.
- Peel onions and cut into rings.
- Put all the ingredients and the olive oil in a salad bowl and mix.
- Finally, season the salad with salt and pepper and place it on a plate.

Tuna with vegetables and avocado

Nutritional Facts

Time: 15 min

- kcal: 372
- KH: 8 g
- E: 18 g
- Q: 29 g

Ingredients

- 1 can of tuna fillets natural, canned
- 1 avocado, hate, fresh
- 50 g paprika, red, fresh
- 50 g paprika, orange, fresh
- 50 g of cucumber
- 1 spring onion / n
- 30 g of sweetcorn canned
- 6 stalks of parsley
- 50 g radishes raw
- ½ peppers (chili) raw
- 1 lime freshly pressed
- 2 tbsp. olive oil

- 1 pinch of nutmeg dried
- 1 pinch of sea salt (Fleur de sel)
- 1 pinch of pepper, black

Preparation

- Open the tuna can a bit and drain the juice, then open the tin completely and cut the tuna into pieces with the fork.
- Halve the avocado and remove the kernel.
- Halve the lime and squeeze the juice.
- Sprinkle both avocado halves with a little lime juice.
- Peel the cucumber and cut it into pieces.
- Remove the peppers from the seeds and partitions and cut into small cubes.
- Wash the tomatoes and cut into pieces.
- Clean the spring onion and cut into rings.
- Pour corn into a sieve and drain
- Wash the parsley and shake it dry, then peel and chop the leaves.
- Chop the chili lengthwise and corer lengthwise, then chop finely.
- Clean the radish and cut into small pieces.
- Put tuna, cucumber, peppers, tomatoes, spring onions, corn, parsley, radishes and chili pepper in a bowl.
- Add olive oil and a little lime juice and season with freshly grated nutmeg, salt and pepper.
- Mix the salad well, then serve together with the avocado.

Colorful vegetable salad

Nutritional Facts

Time: 30 min

- kcal: 239
- KH: 10 g
- E: 4 g
- Q: 19g

Ingredients

- 200 g aubergine raw
- 150 g of tomato / n
- 40 g paprika, yellow, fresh
- 40 g paprika, red, fresh
- 25 g of endives salad
- 25 g Romanosalat
- 1 small onion, red
- 1 small pepper (chili) raw
- 2 cloves of garlic
- 1 pinch of cumin
- 1 pinch of sea salt (Fleur de sel)
- 1 pinch of pepper, black

- 4 tablespoons olive oil

Preparation

- Wash eggplant and dry, then cut into pieces.

- Peel garlic and squeeze with garlic press.

- Mix aubergine with 1 tbsp. olive oil, garlic, salt and pepper in a bowl and spread on a baking sheet lined with baking paper.

- Eggplant for about 10 minutes at 160 ° Cook C in a preheated oven until soft.

- Meanwhile, wash and quarter the tomatoes.

- Remove peppers from cores and partitions and cut into thin sticks.

- Wash lettuce leaves and shake dry, then cut into thin strips.

- Peel onion and cut into strips.

- Cut chilli pepper into thin rings.

- Mix tomatoes, peppers, lettuce, onion and chili pepper in a salad bowl.

- Add the olive oil, cumin, salt and pepper and mix well.

- Take the aubergine out of the oven, allow cooling briefly and adding to the salad.

- Mix everything and place it on two plates.

Chickpea salad with tomatoes and cucumber

Nutritional Facts

Time: 10 min

- kcal: 153
- KH: 10 g
- E: 4 g
- F: 10g

Ingredients

- 100 g of tomatoes
- 50 g of chickpeas
- 60 g of cucumber
- 10 g spring onion
- 1 tbsp olive oil
- Sea-salt
- Pepper

Preparation

- Wash tomatoes and cut them into pieces.
- Chickpeas in a colander and rinse under running water, then drain.
- Wash cucumber and cut it into pieces.

- Clean spring onion and cut it into rings.

- Place tomatoes, chickpeas, cucumber and spring onion in a salad bowl.

- Add olive oil and season with salt and pepper.

- Mix the salad and put it in a bowl.

Beef steak with broccoli

Nutritional Facts

Time: 20 min

- kcal: 430
- KH: 9 g
- E: 39g
- Q: 24 g

Ingredients

- 120 g beef fillet
- 60 g of broccoli
- 30 g pepper, red, fresh
- 2 cloves of garlic
- 1 onion, red
- 1 stalk of basil fresh
- 1 stalk of rosemary
- 2 tbsp. olive oil
- 1 pinch of sea salt (Fleur de sel)
- 1 pinch of pepper, black

Preparation

- Wash the peppers and cut them into strips.

- Peel the onion and cut it into rings.

- Peel and finely chop the garlic.

- Wash the herbs and shake dry, peel the leaves from the basil and chop.

- Wash the broccoli and cut the florets from the stem.

- Add the broccoli to a pot of water and steam, bring the water to a boil and cook the vegetables with the lid closed for 5 to 8 minutes.

- Wash beef filet and dab dry.

- Heat the olive oil in the pan and add the filet with rosemary together.

- Fry the filet for 3 - 5 minutes, depending on the thickness and desired cooking point, then remove, salt and pepper and let rest briefly.

- Meanwhile, add the pepper, onion and garlic to the hot pan and sauté.

- Season with salt and pepper.

- Arrange broccoli, pate and beef fillet on a plate.

- Place the basil over the meat and serve.

Chicken thighs with vegetables

Nutritional Facts

Time: 60 min

- kcal: 615
- KH: 6 g
- E: 35g
- F: 48 g

Ingredients

- 4 chicken drumsticks, with skin and bones
- 100 g cherry tomatoes
- 100 g mushrooms, brown
- 1 onion
- 6 tbsp. olive oil
- 4 garlic toes
- 2 stalks of rosemary
- 1 teaspoon paprika, powder
- 1 pinch of sea salt
- 1 pinch of pepper, black

Preparation

- Wash the chicken drumsticks and pat dry.
- Peel the onion and cut it into rings.

- Wash the rosemary and shake it dry.

- Crush the garlic cloves with the flat side of the knife.

- Rub the chicken drumsticks all over with olive oil, paprika, salt and pepper.

- Then place the thighs together with onion and garlic in a fireproof mold and place the rosemary on them.

- Boil thighs in a preheated oven at 200 ° C for 30 minutes.

- While doing so, wash and halve the tomatoes.

- Clean and slice the mushrooms.

- Add both after 30 minutes to the thighs and cook everything for another 10 - 15 minutes until the thighs are cooked.

- Then serve the chicken drumsticks hot in the pan.

Quinoa with roasted pumpkin

Nutritional Facts

Time: 30 min

- kcal: 266
- KH: 32 g
- E: 7 g
- Q: 11 g

Ingredients

- 60g quinoa
- 200 g Hokkaido pumpkin
- ½ onion
- 50 g rocket
- 1 sprig of fresh mint
- Juice of half a lime
- 2 tbsp. olive oil
- Pepper
- Sea-salt

Preparation

- Place the quinoa in a fine sieve and rinse under running water to rinse off the bitter substances.

- Cover the quinoa in a saucepan with water. Simmer for 8 - 10 minutes until the granules are firm.

- Drain the quinoa and allow evaporating.

- Wash and dry the pumpkin, then cut in half and scrape out the seeds with a spoon.

- Cut the pumpkin into small pieces.

- Peel the onion, halve and cut it into thin rings.

- Wash the rocket and drain well.

- Heat the oil in the pan and sauté the pumpkin.

- Add the quinoa and onion and season with salt and pepper.

- Wash the mint and shake dry, peel off the leaves and chop.

Add the lime juice, rocket and mint and mix everything together.

Dessert & snacks

VEGAN SNAKE RECIPES

It is mid-morning and you're feeling a little peckish - what will you eat? You feel a bit deprived because you are on the vegan diet, and you can't think of any tasty and fast snack ideas. Or perhaps you've just come home from work and are craving a yummy treat, but you are tired. You, therefore, want your vegan snack to be easy, hassle-free, and not one of the most complicated time-consuming recipes on the planet, even better - preferably just something that you can throw together in under 5 or 10 minutes.

Below is a list of some tasty, fast and easy vegan snacks recipes and food ideas to help make your life a little easier.

Popcorn

It's a tasty, rather low-calorie snack that can be ready to eat in under 10 minutes. It's perfect if you're craving something a little salty.

Nutritional Facts

Servings per container   5

Prep Total	10 min
Serving Size	8

Amount per serving	
Calories	0%
	% Daily Value
Total Fat 3g	20%
Saturated Fat 4g	32%
Trans Fat 2g	2%
Cholesterol	2%
Sodium 110mg	0.2%
Total Carbohydrate 21g	50%
Dietary Fiber 9g	1%
Total Sugar 1g	1%
Protein 1g	
Vitamin C 7mcg	17%
Calcium 60mg	1%
Iron 7mg	10%
Potassium 23mg	21%

Ingredient:

- Place 2 tablespoons of olive oil and ¼ cup popcorn in a large saucepan.
- Cover with a lid, and cook the popcorn over a medium flame, ensuring that you are shaking it constantly. Just when you think that it's not working, keep on enduring for another minute or two, and the popping will begin.
- When the popping stops, take off from the heat and place it in a large bowl.

- Add plenty of salt to taste, and if desired, dribble in ¼ cup to ½ cup of melted coconut oil. If you are craving sweet popcorn, add some maple syrup to the coconut oil, about ½ cup, or to taste.

5 Minutes or Less Vegan Snacks

Here's a list of basically 'no-preparation required' vegan snack ideas that you can munch on anytime:

Nutritional Facts

Servings per container   5

Prep Total	10 min
Serving Size	8
Amount per serving	
Calories	0%
	% Daily Value
Total Fat 20g	190%
Saturated Fat 2g	32%
Trans Fat 1g	2%
Cholesterol	2%
Sodium 70mg	0.2%
Total Carbohydrate 32g	150%
Dietary Fiber 8g	1%
Total Sugar 1g	1%
Protein 3g	
Vitamin C 7mcg	17%
Calcium 210mg	1%

Iron 4mg	10%
Potassium 25mg	20%

Ingredients:

- Trail mix: nuts, dried fruit, and vegan chocolate pieces.

- Fruit pieces with almond butter, peanut butter or vegan chocolate spread

- Frozen vegan cake, muffin, brownie or slice that you made on the weekend

- Vegetable sticks (carrots, celery, and cucumber, etc.) with a Vegan Dip (homemade or store-bought) such as hummus or beetroot dip. (Careful of the store-bought ingredients though).

- Smoothie - throw into the blender anything you can find (within limits!) such as soy milk, coconut milk, rice milk, almond milk, soy yogurt, coconut milk yogurt, cinnamon, spices, sea salt, berries, bananas, cacao powder, vegan chocolate, agave nectar, maple syrup, chia seeds, flax seeds, nuts, raisins, sultanas... What you put into your smoothie is up to you, and you can throw it all together in less than 5 minutes!

- Crackers with avocado, soy butter, and tomato slices, or hummus spread.

- Pack of chips (don't eat them too often). There are many vegan chip companies that make kale chips, corn chips, potato chips, and vegetable chips, so enjoy a small bowl now and again.

Fresh Fruit

The health benefits of eating fresh fruit daily should not be minimized. So, make sure that you enjoy some in-season fruit as one of your daily vegan snacks.

Nutritional Facts

Servings per container	10
Prep Total	10 min
Serving Size	5/5
Amount per serving	
Calories	1%
	% Daily Value
Total Fat 24g	2%
Saturated Fat 8g	3%
Trans Fat 4g	2%
Cholesterol	2%
Sodium 10mg	22%
Total Carbohydrate 7g	54%
Dietary Fiber 4g	1%
Total Sugar 1g	1%
Protein 1g	24
Vitamin C 2mcg	17%

Calcium 270mg	15%
Iron 17mg	20%
Potassium 130mg	2%

Ingredients:

- Chop your favorite fruit and make a fast and easy fruit salad, adding some squeezed orange juice to make a nice juicy dressing.
- Serve with some soy or coconut milk yogurt or vegan ice-cream if desired, and top with some tasty walnuts or toasted slivered almonds to make it a sustaining snack.

Vegan Cake

If you are tired or very busy during the week, I recommend you set aside a few hours on the weekends to do your baking. Bake one or two yummy vegan snack recipes to last you the week and freeze them in portions. Find some easy (or gourmet if you wish) vegan cake recipes, muffin recipes, brownie recipes or slice recipes that look delicious, and that you know will satisfy your snack cravings during the week.

Vegan Health Slice

Once again, if you bake it on the weekends, you will not have to prepare your morning and afternoon tea during the week. There are so many delicious recipes nowadays for vegan health slices. There's an apple-crumble slice, oat and nut slice, dried-fruit slice, blueberry slice, chocolate-brownie slice, and so many more delicious recipes! Why not bake a different vegan slice every weekend? This will keep your vegan snacks from becoming boring.

As you can see, your vegan snacks can be very fast and easy to prepare. And it's always a very good habit to get into to do your vegan baking on the weekend so that your mid-week snacks can be hassle-free!

Spicy Apple Crisp

Nutritional Facts

Servings per container	5
Prep Total	10 min
Serving Size	7
Amount per serving	
Calories	0.2%
	% Daily Value
Total Fat 8g	22%
Saturated Fat 1g	51%
Trans Fat 0g	2%
Cholesterol	2%
Sodium 20mg	0.2%
Total Carbohydrate 70g	540%
Dietary Fiber 3g	1%
Total Sugar 6g	1%
Protein 6g	24
Vitamin C 4mcg	170%
Calcium 160mg	12%

Iron 2mg	210%
Potassium 30mg	21%

Ingredients:

- 8 cooking apples
- 4 oz. or 150 g flour
- 7 oz. or 350 g brown sugar
- 5 oz. or 175 g vegan butter
- ¼ tablespoon ground cinnamon
- ¼ tablespoon ground nutmeg
- Zest of one lemon
- 1 tablespoon fresh lemon juice

Instructions:

- Peel, quarter and core cooking apples.
- Cut apple quarters into thin slices and place them in a bowl.
- Blend nutmeg and cinnamon then sprinkle over apples.
- Sprinkle with lemon rind.
- Add lemon juice and toss to blend.
- Arrange slices in a large baking dish.
- Make a mixture of sugar, flour and vegan butter in a mixing bowl then put over apples, smoothing it over.
- Place the dish in the oven.
- Bake at 370°F, 190°C or gas mark 5 for 60 minutes, until browned and apples are tender.

Apple Cake

Nutritional Facts

Servings per container   8

Prep Total	10 min
Serving Size	2
Amount per serving	
Calories	0%
	% Daily Value
Total Fat 4g	210%
Saturated Fat 3g	32%
Trans Fat 2g	2%
Cholesterol	8%
Sodium 300mg	0.2%
Total Carbohydrate 20g	50%
Dietary Fiber 1g	1%
Total Sugar 1g	1%
Protein 3g	
Vitamin C 1mcg	18%
Calcium 20mg	1%
Iron 8mg	12%

Potassium 70mg	21%

Ingredients:

- 2 oz. or 50 g flour
- 3 tablespoon baking powder
- ½ tablespoon of salt
- 2 tablespoon vegan shortening
- ¼ pint or 125 ml unsweetened soya milk
- 4 or 5 apples
- 4 oz. or 110 g sugar
- 1 tablespoon cinnamon

Instructions:

- Sift together flour, baking powder, and salt.
- Add shortening and rub in very lightly.
- Add milk slowly to make soft dough and mix.
- Place on floured board and roll out ½ inch or 1 cm thick.
- Put into shallow greased pan.
- Wash, pare, core and cut apples into sections; press them into the dough.
- Sprinkle with sugar and dust with cinnamon.
- Bake at 375°F, 190°C or gas mark 5 for 30 minutes or until apples are tender and brown.
- Serve with soya cream.

Apple Charlotte

Nutritional Facts

Servings per container	**5**
Prep Total	10 min
Serving Size	4
Amount per serving	
Calories	60%
	% Daily Value
Total Fat 1g	200%
Saturated Fat 20g	3%
Trans Fat 14g	2%
Cholesterol	2%
Sodium 210mg	2%
Total Carbohydrate 7g	210%
Dietary Fiber 1g	9%
Total Sugar 21g	8%
Protein 4g	
Vitamin C 4mcg	22%
Calcium 30mg	17%

Iron 8mg	110%
Potassium 12mg	2%

Ingredients:

- 2 lbs. or 900 g good cooking apples
- 4 oz. or 50 g almonds (chopped)
- 2 oz. or 50 g currants and sultanas mixed
- 1 stick cinnamon (about 3 inches or 7 cm long)
- Juice of ½ a lemon
- Whole bread (cut very thinly) spread
- Sugar to taste.

Instructions:

- Pare, core, and cut up the apples.
- Stew the apples with a teacupful of water and the cinnamon, until the apples have become a pulp.
- Remove the cinnamon, and add sugar, lemon juice, the almonds, and the currants and sultanas (previously picked, washed, and dried).
- Mix all well and allow the mixture to cool.
- Grease a pie-dish and line it with thin slices of bread and butter,
- Then place on it a layer of apple mixture, repeat the layers, finishing with slices of bread and vegan butter.
- Bake at 375°F, 190°C or gas mark 5 for 45 minutes.

Vegan Brownie

Nutritional Facts

Servings per container	**3**
Prep Total	10 min
Serving Size	7
Amount per serving	
Calories	20%
	% Daily Value
Total Fat 3g	22%
Saturated Fat 22g	8%
Trans Fat 17g	21%
Cholesterol	20%
Sodium 120mg	70%
Total Carbohydrate 30g	57%
Dietary Fiber 4g	8%
Total Sugar 10g	8%
Protein 6g	
Vitamin C 1mcg	1%
Calcium 20mg	31%
Iron 2mg	12%
Potassium 140mg	92%

Ingredients:

- 1/2 cup non-dairy butter melted

- 5 tablespoons cocoa
- 1 cup granulated sugar
- 3 teaspoons Ener-G egg replacer
- 1/4 cup water
- 1 teaspoon vanilla
- 3/4 cup flour
- 1 teaspoon baking powder
- 1/2 teaspoon salt
- 1/2 cup walnuts (optional)

Instructions:

- Heat oven to 350°. Prepare an 8" x 8" baking pan with butter or canola oil.
- Combine butter, cocoa, and sugar in a large bowl.
- Mix the egg replacer and water in a blender until frothy.
- Add to the butter mixture with vanilla. Add the flour, baking powder, and salt, and mix thoroughly.
- Add the walnuts if desired. Pour the batter into the pan and spread evenly.

Bake for 40 to 45 minutes, or until a toothpick inserted comes out clean.

FINAL WORDS

Thank you for purchasing this cookbook! This is the 5th book I've written since 2016.

It took me years to write this one, partly because I am a full-time mom and nutritionist. The main reason, however, is that I decided to challenge myself even more this time.

My goal for this guide was to put very complex and technical concepts in the simplest way, so as to make it readable for everyone.

To do what I mentioned above, I accurately selected what I believe are the most useful and effective pieces of advice for you. In my 30 years+ of professional experience I've had the amazing chance to deal with thousands of people of all ages, gender, and personality, and it inevitably has some reflections on my writings.

I don't like to call myself an author, yet I have to admit that I learned a lot while writing books over the past few years. In fact, what I got from those past publications was validation from readers who enjoyed my work and encouraged me to keep writing.

I always value the opinion of readers and take into account criticism as well.

I do believe that reviews are a great way to give someone credit for the work done and I love reading them all the time.

Other readers will do the same before purchasing my books; that's why I give special importance to reviews and I feel bad when getting a bad one.

Anyway, I hope you keep in mind that I am a self-published author, without the huge possibilities that publishing houses have (such as proofreading, special formatting and so on...). However, I hope I accomplished at least the goal I had in my mind - which was to provide you precious information about intermittent fasting, based on scientific studies as well as my own experience, and, most importantly, I hope you learned something new and will act on it to change your life.

Special thanks go to my family, in particular to my beloved husband and my two little daughters, who read this book before than anyone else. I got great feedbacks from them and I am elated about that, even though I think theirs are a little bit biased. After all, they saw me when at nights, often after exhausting workdays, I locked myself up in the study room writing and organizing this guide in the best possible way.

I hope you will keep that in mind too and consider using some seconds of your precious time to leave a review on this book.

I will be GRATEFUL for each one of you.

P.S. I'm a nutritionist, I am a mom, I am a woman but above all... I **am a human being**. An immaculate work is far from possible, especially when you are alone. So, please, if you wish to report any typos or inaccuracies you encountered in this guide, please consider emailing me at teresamoorenutritionist@gmail.com. I will do my best to answer you and make the requested adjustments.

CPSIA information can be obtained
at www.ICGtesting.com
Printed in the USA
BVHW010649220121
598317BV00013B/154

9 781801 582483